THE AUTHENTIC LEADER AS SERVANT (ALS)

ALS II COURSE 1
ADAPTABILITY LEADERSHIP
Attributes, Principles, and Practices

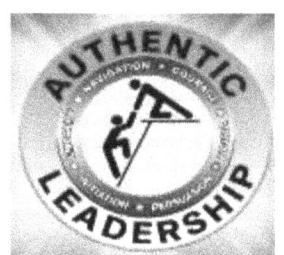

SYLVANUS N. WOSU, Ph.D

THE AUTHENTIC LEADER AS SERVANT
ALS II COURSE 1
Developing Adaptability Leadership Attributes, Principles, and Practices

© Copyright 2024 by Sylvanus N. Wosu Ph.D.

Printed in the United States of America
ISBN: 978-1-7378712-8-6

All rights reserved. No part of this book may be reproduced or transmitted in any form or by any means, electronic or mechanical, including photocopying, recording, or by any information storage and retrieval system, without permission in writing from the copyright owner.

Bible quotations are from the New King James (NKJV) version of the Bible unless otherwise indicated.

Other versions used in this book are the New International Version (NIV), New Living Translation (NLT), King James Version (KJV), English Standard Version (ESV), and Good News Translation (GNT). Unless otherwise specified, NKJV should be assumed.

The views expressed in this work are solely those of the author and do not necessarily reflect the views of the publisher, and the publisher disclaims any responsibility for them.

To order additional copies of this book, contact:
Proisle Publishing Services LLC
39-67 58th Street, 1st floor
Woodside, NY 11377, USA
Phone: (+1 646-480-0129)
info@proislepublishing.com

PROISLE PUBLISHING

TABLE OF CONTENTS

FOREWORD	IX
ACKNOWLEDGMENTS	XIII
DEDICATION	XV
PREFACE	17
About Leader As Servant Leadership (LSL) Model	20
About the Authentic Leader as Servant (ALS)	23
About the ALS Courses	24
CHAPTER 1	
UNDERSTANDING LEADERSHIP ATTRIBUTES	33
Functional Definitions	33
Comparisons With Other Works	38
Principle of Leadership Attribute	40
Authentic Leadership Attributes	41
Summary 1 Understanding Leadership Process	46
CHAPTER 2	
ADAPTABILITY LEADERSHIP ATTRIBUTE	49
Servant Leadership Adaptability Attribute	51
Principle of Leadership Adaptability Attribute	53
Summary 2 Adaptability Leadership Attribute	54
CHAPTER 3	
DEVELOPING ADAPTABILITY–SELF-SECURITY	57
Summary 3 Developing Adaptability–Self-Security	59
CHAPTER 4	
BUILDING ADAPTABILITY–FLEXIBILTY	61
Summary 4 Developing Adaptability–flexibity	63
CHAPTER 5	
DEVELOPING ADAPTABILITY–COMPASSION	65
Summary 5 Developing Adaptability–Compassion	67
TOPIC INDEX	69
REFERENCES	71

FOREWORD

The modern world today is obsessed with standardization and modalities. As a result, in the realm of leadership, many books have spout associated leadership theories and models and explain them as the path to follow. However, the critical dimensions that distinguish the effectiveness of any leadership process are the values and attribute the leader brings to the table; desired change is influenced by leadership styles or standards. These many standards and theories of leadership often are not in step with the changing times or the followers' needs. The trend is a bit like stocking different kinds of foods in a grocery store and expecting that they will meet everybody's needs the same way and at all times. Aisles are packed with varieties of food with expiration dates in the future, but getting the best deal on the products is what really matters to those who buy and use the products

In many ways, this is the state of leadership in the modern world. Increasingly, even leaders of public institutions are tasked with turning a profit for themselves or the organization they serve. The idea of a "leader" seems to float uneasily alongside the ranks of fundraisers or profit raisers in contrast to any kind of role model for followers or employees. That which is knowable, measurable, and marketable has surpassed the difficult intangibility of strong moral leadership attributes as the central guideline for achievement and success.

In this complicated space, Dr. Sylvanus Wosu introduces his complex idea of the Leader as a Servant Leadership, which is in this book, modeled on Christian tradition. Like all intricate ideas, Dr. Wosu's central point depends on a paradox: a person is best qualified to lead when he or she is most ready to serve. This paradox has been monopolized rhetorically by "public servants" who often serve either self-interest or the interests of specific lobbies. The Authentic Leader as Servant penetrates past the superficial concept of "serving" and details the internal state of true servitude or Servanthood.

While the book is primarily focused on the Christian model of leadership attributes such as discipleship, empathy, affection, and Servanthood, it does so not merely on the grounds of blind faith, but rather via numerous contemporary sociological and business-driven studies on how leaders should seek a leader-follower relationship that is simultaneously productive and nurturing. Dr. Wosu's most piercing insights always involve this secular–Christian dialogue. This book demonstrates that Christ's model for leadership is one that may exist successfully outside the confines of a faith relationship; it places the values of Christ's religious significance in leadership at the center of the framework. It is clear from Dr. Wosu's generous own life story of faith—a faith tested by humbling difficulties—is at the center of both his orientation and motivation for writing.

In language that is so concise, it is often illustrated in mathematical formulas; Dr. Wosu explains the deep structural integrity of Christ's Leader as the Servant Leadership model. One could imagine leaders of any doctrine benefiting from the analyses contained in these pages. The book's message repeatedly encourages the reader to imagine a scenario or reflect on memories and personal experiences to prove or test its many points. Thus, the book depends on a form of praxis, a lesson that could be or has been enacted, by the participating reader. I am very impressed at the volume and level of thinking of the author. Parts of the book involve his personal story, which is especially riveting. I cannot imagine what he had to endure, which he referred to as a" wilderness walk," to accomplish the goal he set for himself. His life stories on these pages are inspiring and stimulating.

In this way, the text eschews dogmatism in favor of the self-discovery Socratic Method of teaching and learning. The reader is not badgered into complying with a religious objective but is rather asked to consider the applicability of difficult biblical concepts in relation to modern life. It is a fascinating and very thought-provoking read.

Hence, the book does not seek to make the leader a servant, a cookie-cutter corporate buzzword, but rather asks the reader to imagine him or herself interacting with a range of concepts. One of Dr. Wosu's great strengths is his reservation when it comes to forcing his reading's interpretation on the material he presents.

The book parallels Biblical and modern leadership scenarios in ways that consistently provoke thought, and while it is clear Dr. Wosu has his particular leadership style; the space for the reader's own thoughts is always left open.

The book could not have been written in any other way with integrity. Its format and formulas are offered to the reader of the leader as a servant role that it analyzes in its pages. To find a text that instructs from this humble position is profoundly refreshing in a genre that is often packaged inside a cover with a sizeable picture of the "modest" author, smiling egotistically beneath a name spelled out in large, gold lettering. Throughout its pages, this text feels as if it serves the reader.

In the end, this is the most satisfying aspect of the book. There is no standardized approach to achieving successful leadership. There is no promise of power and a bigger payday; in fact, the book often proffers just the opposite. The reader is not encouraged to devalue the experience of leadership by finding some economic metric for marking success but is rather asked to think deeply about the most basic elements of internal and social interaction within the framework of a Christian tradition. What this means will be different for every reader. Indeed, even in the context of single chapters, I found myself questioning or re-evaluating moments of my own life. This book serves; it doesn't feel like filling in multiple-choice questions, staring at a wall of flavorless grocery products, or hearing the endless servant promises of today's political scene. It feels like a humble invitation to consider a single paradoxical element of a profoundly productive tradition.

-Tobias Bates

Acknowledgments

A book on leadership attributes as aspects of Servant Leadership sprouted from the wealth of knowledge and the inspirations of many other leaders. Their writings were sources of inspiration, challenges, and examples of excellence to emulate. I acknowledge the leaders listed below for their help in one way or the other. I am very grateful and I hereby express my appreciation and thanks:

Mr. Wayne Holt, introduced me first to the subject of Servanthood in one of our Stephen Ministerial Training classes, and he is the one who has conducted his life as a leader–servant; he encouraged me throughout my writing;

Dr. Harvey Borovetz, Distinguished Professor and Chair of the Bioengineering Department, is a leader-servant in many ways, he modeled Servanthood and encouragement attributes throughout his leadership in an academic setting.

Dr. Clifford and Dr. Patience Obih, in so many measures exemplified the practical leadership attributes discussed in this book.

Pastor Lance Lecocq, Lead Pastor of Monroeville Assembly of God, for his excellent model of servanthood, empowerment, and emulation attributes to the ministerial team, I am thankful for his motivation and encouragement throughout the several hours on this project;

To my administrative assistant, Ms. Terri Cook, who was always the first to review the manuscript; I am very grateful for her dedication.

To the African Christian Fellowship USA, institutions, and all other organizations where I have served in one leadership capacity or the other, thank you for affording me senior leadership positions that provided the leadership platform and opportunities to grow as a leader.

Dr. Lawrence Owoputi, a brother I am proud to call my friend; for his dedication to serving others, his generosity, healing care, and responsibility attributes during our term in office and in chapter leadership positions; he taught me that excellent following is also part of good leadership;

To Tobias Bates, for his editorial work on the original draft of the book, and his dedication to completing the work.

Mr. Edward F. Kondis, a member of our Engineering Board of Visitors, for his always encouraging and moral support;

Dr. Enefaa N. Wosu, my wife and life partner, for her love, commitment, and prayer support, especially during those long night hours I was not there for her and her constant reminder of who I must be as a leader-servant. Without her support, forbearance, wisdom, and encouragement, this project would not have been completed; I say, thank you very much.

And to God alone be all the glory and honor for the divine inspiration and guidance in initiating and completing this life-transforming book project.

Dedication

I humbly submit this book back unto the gracious hands of God who inspired the writings through His Holy Spirit!

I dedicate this book to my virtuous wife of 45 years, Rev. (Dr.) Enefaa Wosu whose spiritual leadership is an important gateway to our home, and to our four wonderful children—Prof. Eliada Wosu-Griffin EL, HeCareth, Tamuno-Emi, and Chidinma. From them all, I learnt what it meant to be a leader-servant. I could not be blessed with better teachers.

Preface

What characteristics did Biblical leaders like the Apostle Paul, Moses, Joshua, and Nehemiah as servants of their people display outwardly that distinguished them from other leaders, both then and now? The Apostle Paul kept his focus to *emulate* Christ and endured all the infirmities and persecutions he suffered to complete his goal to preach the gospel of Jesus Christ. He inspired Timothy and others through his effective *discipleship* leadership to imitate him as he emulated Christ. Moses' outward display of his *trus*t in God's power earned him a good level of trust from the people and empowered him for the mission of delivery of God's children from bondage in Egypt; he had to *reproduce* himself in Joshua to complete the mission. But the greatest of them was Jesus Christ, who humbly sacrificed His life to finish the work of redemption. In His *Servanthood*, commitment, and love for the people, He became the ultimate *model* of a leader as a servant to *emulate*.

Let's consider for a moment secular leaders in these current times! For example, think of Henry Ford, who founded the successful Ford Motor Company; Bill Gates who created the global empire that is Microsoft; Albert Einstein, who in many ways is synonymous with a genius for his contributions to modern physics; Abraham Lincoln, remembered as one of the greatest presidents and leaders of United States; and many others like these we cannot mention. What did all these leaders have in common? What propelled them to turn their initial failures or challenges into eventual successes? None had a direct mentor or inherited any fortune from their parents. Nevertheless, they all eventually succeeded. These people can be distinguished from others based on their self-will to succeed, their self-confidence and belief in themselves, their self-determination, and their perseverance, among other characteristics. The distinguishing characteristics displayed externally in service or relationships toward others are the outward functional attributes that define that leader.

Think about yourself as a student, faculty member, or that new executive. What was it that made your journey to success different and even great? Students and colleagues, when they see or hear about my display of what I have referred to as the 'wilderness walk of faith', have asked me to share the critical attitudinal elements that made me remain inwardly resilient and undaunted and yet outwardly joyful in the difficulties I had faced. This book is the result of those reflections. Let me explain one such teaching moment.

Many years ago, sitting in my research lab on a Saturday morning trying to finish writing my dissertation, a fellow graduate student walked into the room to talk with me. He was contemplating terminating his graduate studies. He was a privileged single male student but felt the load was just too much.

"Sylvanus," he asked, with seriousness in his eyes, "your research advisor suggested that I should ask you, 'what is it that makes you tick?'.'What is it about you that makes you joyful and at peace with yourself and determined to finish, no matter the situations and high expectations we face in this department?"

What he asked me were deeply reflective questions, but I was willing and excited to answer them. Even so, before I do, let's look at the context. At that period in my life, I had four little children as a graduate student; in fact, more children than any of the faculties at that time, except for one faculty member who had eight children. I received little or no support from the department. I was then an international alien, did not qualify for financial aid, and was not given any research assistant position. I was, therefore, self-supported with two off-campus part-time jobs. I joked at being a minority of minorities, the only student in the department with such a label,—but I was self-willed to succeed. My adaptability attribute, coupled with perseverance and resilience, was all that I needed to succeed despite the odds against me. In every exam, homework assignment, or project I had to compete with students with full financial aid, plus they had nothing to distract their attention from their studies. I lived with the attitude that using disadvantages as an excuse was not an option. Aspiring to earn my Ph.D. was a life dream, and I was willing to give my ultimate best to actualize that dream even in the face of challenges. The choice was mine!

So I looked at my classmate and all I could see was a student striding through a valley through which I also walked. He needed me to show him how to walk the walk, to empathize with him. To answer his question, I smiled, not that I wanted to, but because it was just who I was. The joy he attributed to me was an overflow of my appreciation of God's grace that His life in me was externally manifesting His light to bless someone else. It was a great teaching moment; I capitalized on it to tell my classmate that my joy was not about me. He could see physically but about He who was in me, he could not see in the flesh; I needed him to know that I was just showing forth His life in me. At first, my classmate did not understand the spiritual prose or metaphor I was using. He looked surprised but open to hearing more.

I did not ask if he was a Christian. However, right on my desk was my small green pocket Bible. I opened to 2 Corinthians 12:9 (NIV) and handed it to him to read. As he read the passage: "But he said to me, 'My grace is sufficient for you, for my power is made perfect in weakness.' Therefore, I will boast all the more gladly about my weaknesses, so that Christ's power may rest on me," I noticed how absorbed he was in the words

He looked astonished and read it again, this time silently. "This is interesting, but what does this mean?" He asked. I took his question to mean, "How does this relate to my question?

I explained to my friend that the external attitudes he or my advisors saw in me that warranted the question, "What makes you tick" were inspired by my inner value system based on my faith in this same Christ and His teachings. My desire to manifest His life and self-confidence is all because of what He has promised in His word if I believed. I have believed His words and have gained self-determination and faith to make the right choices through Him for my life, and his spirit has given me perseverance and resilience to focus on finishing strong in pursuit of any goal. "With that faith, I have continued, more passionately and excitedly; I can look at my challenges and vulnerabilities and delight joyfully in them, even as an alien minority of minorities! His grace and power have empowered me to do all things I want to do. That is what makes me tick," I explained.

He looked at me as if he got his answer. "Wow, thanks!" he said, looking inspired and ready to face his challenges. As we concluded with a prayer, and he stood up to leave, I pointed empathetically to his face and said, "If I made it despite my challenges, you have absolutely no excuse but to persevere to complete your studies; you can make it too!"

It is fitting to report that this encounter with my classmate transformed his will and determination to continue. Yes, he was encouraged and went on to complete his graduate studies. He emulated self-will and perseverance from the example of the most vulnerable of all students in the department.

The inner value system of a Leader-Servant is founded not only on his faith but his self-will, coupled with self-leadership; it is the greatest mentor who can turn any situation into an inconceivable success. Self-will is the primary driver for determination, resilience, and perseverance. It is what wakes you up in the morning to ask for strength to do whatever it is you are setting out to do. Based on my life walk of faith, I can state with absolute certainty that faith is the unseen assuredness that can empower you to turn your life's probable impossibilities into great and improbable possibilities.

ABOUT LEADER AS SERVANT LEADERSHIP (LSL) MODEL

Looking at the testimony above, do you know the source that energizes the characteristics you display outside and how your inner self is related to what others see outside? What distinguishes you from others is what combines to define your attributes! As a follower, can you identify the characteristics that distinguish your leaders? As an executive, how do you base your evaluation of yourself? Or how do you evaluate that brand-new manager or new youth director you want to hire? To what do you compare the individual's qualities when you look at his CV? What is the basis of your measure? Do you know if you are a substantial leader? These personal questions and much more are the subjects of this two-volume book, 'The Authentic Leader as Servant Part I: The Outward Leadership Attributes, Principles, and Practices', is written in two parts; the second part 'The Leader as Servant Leadership Model. Part II'; deals with the Inner Strength Leadership Attributes, Principles, and Practices.

When we think about today's corporate greed, deepening divide between the haves and have-not, gridlock in political systems, conflicts and wars, high divorce rates, and the rich young ruler in the Bible, it is easy to agree that all these people share a few things in common: self-centeredness, pride, lack of compassion, and greed. There is a great need in today's suffering world for leader-servants who display leadership attributes. These attributes should be oriented toward selfless service to others. Indeed, our world is increasingly drifting away from global serving reality toward the self and apathy. The most credible message or model for a possible solution to this dilemma and the answer to several complex leadership questions can be found in the foundation of the ultimate leader-servant, Jesus Christ. This book defines the Leader as Servant Leadership attribute as the combined acts of two or more distinctive functional leadership characteristics exhibited in service and relationship toward others. There is no better time than now for a book that presents comprehensive and irrevocable facts and principles regarding how to develop effective attributes of the leader-servant.

The Leader as Servant Leadership Model

My first book on this subject, The Leader as Servant Leadership Model, explains that Jesus' servant leadership model is based on the notion of a Leader as a Servant and not on a Servant as Leader. There are four distinct differences between a Servant as Leader (Servant-leader) and the Leader as Servant (leader--servant) models. It is pertinent to highlight them here to connect to this book, Authentic Leader as Servant.

A Leader as Servant is a leader first. The leader–servant as a leader does not in the line of duty go projecting or lording his or her power and authority over others but is the person to lead the process of influencing desired changes in others through his humble example of being a servant or having a serviceable attitude toward others. He or she is a serving leader, not a lording leader. He leads as a servant by putting others' needs above his own needs and rights. Jesus emphasized the word "as" meaning that the leader (the Master) chooses to serve as a servant even though he is the leader. A leader–servant emulates Jesus, who gave up all rights, and emptied and expended Himself on His followers. He empowered them to become more like Him. A leader-servant is known as a leader first but is seen as a great leader by his humble attendant heart and acts of service to others. His greatness comes from his ability to put others above himself.

Leader as Servant is a Biblical Concept. The model or image of a humble serving leader motivated Jesus' disciples to see that if their master could do this for them, they must also be able to do it for others. Jesus clearly demonstrated the process of leader-as-servant leadership. In some cases, He chose to serve by leading when He wanted to create the image or model of the leader-servant in certain acts. In other cases, He chose to lead by serving, when he showed care and empathy toward the people and led the disciples to see empathy as a leadership attribute.

Leader as Servant is an Authentic Leadership Model to follow. The Leader as the Servant leadership model intentionally positions Jesus as an original model of a leader to follow.

He was serving His disciples to demonstrate that the process of becoming a great leader was earned through humble acts of service to others; He made them understand that He was empowering them to succeed Him as leader-servants through service to others. The result was an incomparable legacy of leadership that changed their communities. The fact that Jesus relinquished his rights or shared His power did not diminish His power and influence. In fact, his influence increased at least 11 X 100%, if we ignore the one case of Judas.

The Leader as Servant Transforms Organizational Culture. The proposed LSL model seeks to transform and sustain the community or organization by instilling key leadership values or "leadership presence" among followers or an organization's members. Change is sustained when everyone in the organization takes ownership of the change. Rather than focusing on leading more followers to be great followers who conform to the organizational culture, LSL seeks to lead and empower better leaders to be distinguished leaders and community builders.

There are four distinctions, which clearly differentiate many of the existing servants as Leader-based philosophies in relation to servant leadership from my LSL model. Even in the corporate or institutional worlds, there is nothing better than Jesus on which to base Servant Leadership. There is nothing more authentic and impacting than the servant leadership modeled by the life and teachings of Jesus Christ.

The LSL model uses exploratory questions, scenarios, and graphic visualizations to excite critical thinking in ways no other book on this subject has yet attempted. Several personal testimonies of my wilderness walk of faith with God are used to connect the reader to real-life experiences of the concepts discussed. The riveting effect is that the text engages and encourages the reader to walk through the experiences presented. The aim is to inspire the reader spiritually, mentally, and professionally with this far-reaching exposition on the subject of servant leadership.

ABOUT THE AUTHENTIC LEADER AS SERVANT (ALS)

The *Authentic Leader as Servant* argues that no leadership model is as authentic, other-centered, able to build communities, and productive and service-oriented as the model of our ultimate leader-servant, Jesus Christ. No source can provide a better point of reference than that provided in the Bible. Hence, this book aims to be more than just a text on leadership; it hopes to be a personal discovery for those who aspire to develop effective leadership attributes that grow leaders as servants who ultimately develop thriving other-centered communities. This book presents a comprehensive, biblically-based study regarding how to develop these attributes and how they are applied in a servant leadership process. In this biblical context and for clarity, Servant Leadership means *Leader-as-Servant Leadership*. A *leader-servant* refers to a *leader as a servant*, which is distinct from a servant-leader or servant as leader.

Leader as Servant Leadership attributes are shaped by the Leadership's Inner Value system, which consists of character, motivation, and commitment. The *Authentic Leader as Servant* is presented as a necessary resource to complement my *The Leader as Servant Leadership (LSL) Model*. The LSL model integrates a transformative leadership framework and interactive dimensions of Servant Leadership. Leader as Servant Leadership is a process in which a leader, in his leadership position, purposefully chooses to put others' rights and needs above his positional rights and personal needs. He then serves, enables, and empowers followers for growth that builds a thriving organization. The LSL model looks at the predominant Servant Leadership concepts and shares how they compare with biblical principles on how we should lead and be led.

ABOUT THE ALS COURSES

The three books, *LSL Model* and *The Authentic Leader as Servant (*Parts I and II), together demonstrate that with today's global visions to reach people of all races and cultures, now is the time for an authentic servant's heart of service. Those visions and the leadership processes are most effective with the appropriate leadership attributes centered more on people than on the organization, principles regarding how to develop effective attributes of leader-servant.

The ALS I and II combined presented twenty leaders as servant leadership attributes. The series of ALS courses supply training guide to understand, develop, and practice the attributes in a leadership process. Each course is independent and self-contained and does not depend on completing any other course in the series of 20 courses. It is, however strongly recommended, in fact a must read, that chapters 1 and 2 in each series be covered as they lay the foundation of LSL model on which ALS is based.

ALS (Parts I & II) Course Layout

The *Authentic Leader as Servant (ALS)* leadership (parts I and II) book has been broken down into 20 courses in workbook format to achieve three goals 1) Self-discovery of the acts of developing the attribute under review in the course, 2) deeper understanding of the principles, research and biblical teaching behind the attributes, and 3) Learning the strategies for practicing the attributes.

Instruction

The set of questions following each chapter are designed to serve as a guide to discover, explore, and practice the essential ALS leadership attributes, principles, and practices in leadership process. The questions are comprehensive review based on the content of this specific chapter only.

To maximize the learning outcomes, the learner must read through this chapter and sections. Some referenced scriptures in the book are repeated in the summaries for added review if needed, even though they were discussed in the section in which they apply.

Chapter 1
Understanding Leadership Attributes

> The exercises that follow each chapter will help you in not only understanding your own strength and weaknesses in your acts of the attribute but will guide you in developing practical strategies you can apply in self-leadership process or helping others grow in leadership
>
> All answers to the questions are contained in the associated chapter or sections; consultation of new sources, except for the reference scriptures, is not needed. Thus, it is expected that you answer the questions after you have read the associated section or chapter of the workbook. The scripture or other references cited are only for references as they already discussed in the book

ALS II Course 1: Adaptability Leadership Attribute—*Flexibility overcomes rigidity in new and changing situations.*

Adaptability is framed as an inner strength quality of a leader in responding to changing needs or situations in a service mission. According to the Army training Handbook, adaptability is "an individual's ability to recognize changes in the environment, identify the critical elements of the new situation, and trigger changes accordingly to meet new requirements." God showed Moses adaptability when he empowered him to use the rod in his hand as an instrument for the mission ahead of him. This course will attempt to give meanings to personal reflective questions to discover the distinguishing characteristics of Leadership Adaptability. Numerous techniques, personal examples, empirical case studies, and applications of the adaptability developing strategies are discussed concepts. Practice questions at the end of each chapter are used to guide your development and to frame meanings out of the content to improve your acts of adaptability in a leadership process.

ALS II Course 2: Courage Leadership Attribute—*Courage is the inner strength of the mind to triumph over paralyzing fears of purposeful action that yields good success*

Courage Leadership Attribute is the lynchpin of effective Servant Leadership that supports the display of all the other attributes? Having the inner strength of character and convictions to persevere and hold on to new and often misunderstood ideas in the face of opposition takes courage—inner strength to triumph over the fear of failure or danger. It is even greater courage to venture into positions or overcome situations that nobody like you, has gone to before or where many better qualified than you had gone and failed. In all cases, they all display courage in the face of obstacles and uncertainties. The success is more about courage than the experience. Can such courage be learned or inspired? How do leaders or successful people in their callings get to their heights of achievements? How can courage be an inner strength within or beyond leadership? How does courage attribute triumph over paralyzing fear? This course explores answers to these questions and more by searching for the distinguishing characteristics of courage. Numerous techniques, personal examples, empirical case studies, including practice questions at the end of each chapter are used to guide your development and to frame meanings out of the content to improve your acts of courage leadership process.

ALS II Course 3: Empathy Leadership Attribute—*A measure of a leader's compassion is the empathic engagement in a follower's experience and state of well-being beyond just expressions of feelings and concerns.*

Empathy attribute is the ability to project one's personality and experiences into another person's thoughts, emotions, direct experience, position, and act toward the wellness of that person. How can a leader walk along with someone in that individual's "wilderness" state of suffering or danger? What motivates a leader to *empathize* with a follower? How is empathy an inner strength leadership attribute? Whether it's in your church, your business, your institution, or in your community, this course provides a comprehensive biblical-based discussion on the role of a leader as a servant in empathizing with those he leads. The aim is to inspire the reader spiritually, mentally, and professionally with this far-reaching exposition on empathy in servant leadership. How can a leader make a lasting positive impact in the lives of those he or she leads? Answers to these and other personal reflective questions are explored in this course on Leadership Empathy Attributes. Numerous techniques, personal examples, empirical case studies, including practice questions at the end of each chapter are used to guide your development and to frame meanings out of the content to improve your acts of empathy leadership process.

ALS II Course 4: Encouragement Leadership Attribute—*The direct measures of encouragement are the inspired strength and quality of uplifted spirit to persevere toward a desired outcome.*

There are times when people want to grow in their potential, want to change their present situation, feel emotionally low in lived experiences, or feel as if they should be appreciated for a job well done. In any of these cases, some encouragement goes a long way to lift up the spirit of someone low. A case study is of the leadership qualities of Barnabas, named the "Son of Encouragement" by the disciples (Acts 4:36), because they saw him as an *encourager*. You can only be an encourager from the strength of your inner personality. The act of encouragement is mostly expressed or *given* to inspire growth or apply a spiritual gift to serve others. What did the disciples see in Barnabas? Obviously, he must have affected them with his acts of encouragement. They saw him as an encourager by his *courage* to *inspire* them at a time they desperately needed to move the ministry forward. This course explores the distinguishing characteristics of encouragement attributes in servant leadership. Each characteristic of encouragement attribute will be discussed in detail with emphasis on strategies of how they can be further developed or practiced by a leader-servant in a leadership process. Practice questions at the end of each chapter are used to guide your development and to frame meanings out of the content to improve your acts of encouragement leadership process.

ALS II Course 5: Initiation Leadership Attribute—*Initiation creates the catalyst for a vision, and the vision when acted upon, produces a desired change.*

The initiation of a process for a desired change is the core of the inner strength of a decisive leader in any leadership process. Initiation leadership is the act of taking step to originate or get something started. In general, initiative is an "individual's action that begins a process, often done without direct managerial influence." The primary outcome of the initiation attribute is that it leads to desired change; something new in the lives of the followers or organization, such as a new growth in followers, a new product or policy in an organization, or a new mission or mission agenda. How do leaders take action to begin a process of change? What are the distinguishing initiation characteristics of leaders such as Moses and Nehemiah in working according to God's agenda? How does a leader conceive a strategic vision for initiation action?. or negotiate his way to influence possible actions toward that vision. This course explores answers to these, and other questions based on examples from Nehemiah (Nehemiah 1:4 through 2:6-8) and Moses and God (Exodus 3 and 4:1-14).

ALS II Course 6: Listening Communication Leadership Attribute
—*Effective communication occurs at the convergence of listening attention, hearing, and understanding of the information transmitted.*

A leader-servant face three important types of communication at one point or the other. At the core is listening ability as the inner strength and ability to receive and understand the meanings of words and messages internally and accurately in a two-way communication process. How does a leader-servant communication with God, the Holy Spirit, and followers (individually or collectively) to be most effective. The course explores how the three elements—words spoken, unspoken, and in the spirit—offer unique reflections of the communication process and what they share in common. How does listening serve as a critical element of effective communication between people forms the bridge by which a leader can be effective?. A leader's capacity to listen to communicate effectively depends on the leader's inner strength to perceive, hear, and understand the information from written, verbal, and non-verbal exchanges. Each characteristic of listening communications attribute will be discussed in detail with emphasis on strategies of how they can be further developed or practiced by a leader-servant. Practice questions at the end of each chapter are used to guide your development and to frame meanings out of the content to improve your acts of listening leadership process.

ALS II Course 7: Navigation Leadership Attribute—*Leaders who prepare for and chart through a purposeful course of action arrive with their followers at the desired destination.*

The navigation attribute is having a *vision* for the intended destination plus the direction to get there. Having a vision is a quality of the inner strength of a leader and the path that the leader follows in the life journey is often influenced by internal and external factors. The organizational culture and climate collectively combine to make an organization unique through the

CHAPTER 1
UNDERSTANDING LEADERSHIP ATTRIBUTES

diversity of employees' characteristics, values, needs, attitudes, and expectations. How does a leader-servant *navigate* and *negotiate* his actions through the organization and people he serves, individually or collectively, to *finish* or *arrive* at his purpose? How do you prepare your followers to *finish* strong or *arrive* at their destinations? This course explores answers to these and other questions and how a leader's inner strength capacity can empower him to navigate the cultural bridges to influence the desired change in others in their personal and professional needs and attitudes.

ALS II Course 8: Responsibility Leadership Attribute—*Leadership responsibility is the measure of the quality of a Leader's accountability for the growth of followers and the organization*

Responsibility leadership refers to possessing the capability and accountability needed in the act of being responsible (trustworthy, dependable, honest, etc.) in a leadership process. At a personal level, it defines the level of your position (pastor, deacon, department head, janitor, etc.) in your church, family, or employment. Responsible leaders in their positions *choose* to emphasize the positive, uplifting, and flourishing side of organizational life. Are there qualities in your position that need to be trained or developed to influence positive outcomes in people and organizations? Organizationally, what are the attributes of the leadership structure, process, and culture that are most conducive for maximizing the growth of followers and organizations in service toward others? How can responsibility qualities be developed to enhance high-quality relationships, emotional competencies, positive communication, beneficial energy development, and positive climates for the effective leader as a servant leadership process? The course explores answers to these and other questions. Distinguishing leadership characteristics of responsibility attributes are identified and discussed in detail. Practice questions at the end of each chapter are used to guide your development and to frame meanings out of the content to improve your acts of responsibility leadership process.

ALS II Course 9: Stewardship Leadership Attribute—*A measure of good stewardship is the entrustments' better and richer growth change at the end than at the beginning*

ALS ADAPTABILITY LEADERSHIP
ATTRIBUTES, PRINCIPLES & PRINCIPLES

*Stewardship leadership is the process of u*tilizing and managing the resources entrusted to you by someone. We recognize that God has ownership of everything above, and below the earth. In that context, we are all stewards of what God owns, including our lives but entrusted to us to be managed and maintained in a purposeful manner that will honor God. What are the distinctive servant leadership characteristics of stewardship and how can they be developed? This course explores answers to these questions with reference to servant leadership. Practice questions at the end of each chapter are used to guide your development and to frame meanings out of the content to improve your acts of steward leadership process

ALS II Course 10: Vision Leadership Attribute—*You have a vision when you understand how you get to your mission-purpose and what the future outcome will be relative to your present.*

The vision leadership attribute gives the leader the ability to specify in the present *what* each follower's or group's growth should be in the future, *where* to focus these efforts to meet that growth; *how* he will accomplish all aspects of his mission, *which* future (destination) he aspires to lead the people, and *when* the purpose will be achieved. Leadership without direction leads followers to nowhere. Vision is the most common descriptor of effective leadership and must be clear and inspirational in order to achieve desired purpose. What are the qualities a visionary leader? When was the last time you added brand new challenges to your normal routine to achieve a new you? Answers to these and other questions are explored in this course. The primary characteristics of visionary leadership will be identified and used to frame a principle of leadership vision attribute. Practice questions at the end of each chapter are used to guide your development and to frame meanings out of the content to improve your acts of encouragement leadership process.

Referenced Scriptures

A variety of Bible translations from over 11,200 original Hebrew, Aramaic, and Greek words to about 6,000 English words do exist with variations in meanings and emphases. I am not a biblical scholar and do not pretend to be one; Hence, I have avoided researching the roots of these words and personally prefer New King James Version (NKJV). I have intentionally used other translations for three main reasons; first, to allow for increased impact and alignment of words to the most desired meaning and emphasis in the concepts being addressed. Second, I wanted new and personal discovery of meanings from translations with which I have not been familiar. And third, I wanted to allow readers who may desire translations other than the NKJV the benefit of their preferred translations. Hence, in addition to the NKJV, other translations used in the book include New International Version (NIV), New Living Translation (NLT), King James Version (KJV), English Standard Version (ESV), and Good News Translation (GNT). Unless otherwise specified, NKJV should be assumed.

Sylvanus Nwakanma Wosu

CHAPTER 1
UNDERSTANDING LEADERSHIP ATTRIBUTES

Leadership attribute is the combined acts of two or more distinctive functional leadership characteristics exhibited in service and relationship toward others.

The starting point of our discussion is the understanding of the key functional definitions and concepts that describe the theme of this book. In general, I will define leadership as an integrative process in which a person applies appropriate attributes to guide and influence the sought-after attitudinal changes in others toward accomplishing a particular goal. Specifically, the Leader as Servant Leadership is a process in which a leader intentionally chooses to put the follower's rights and needs above his positional rights and personal needs, and serves, enables, and empowers them for desired spiritual and professional growth that builds thriving communities.

FUNCTIONAL DEFINITIONS

In the context of these definitions, I will begin the descriptions of the leadership attributes of an authentic leader-servant by offering a functional definition of Leadership Attributes, and showing how that definition differs from those of Leadership Character, Characteristics, and Traits.

Leadership Character is the sum total of personal qualities in leadership, such as honesty, values, vision, trust, and so on that make up the moral capital of the leader; Leadership character should describe who the leader is inside or the leader's basic personality traits.

The Leadership Characteristics describe the distinctive characteristics or features of a leader, such as attitudes, competencies, skills, and specific experiences that go beyond his character (personality). Leadership characteristics determine how (through skills and competencies) the leader leads or take actions in the process of leadership in any particular situation;

The Leadership traits are the distinguishing leadership characteristics of a leader (these are things that define his leadership characteristics), which differentiate from personality traits... Leadership traits are the set of characteristics that define a particular leader's leadership. This means that a leadership characteristic is a trait when it is a unique characteristic of the leader.

Leadership Attributes, unlike leadership character, characteristics, and traits, is *a leadership attribute and the combined act of two or more distinctive functional leadership characteristics exhibited in service and relationship toward others* or traits externally displayed in action toward others. All leadership attributes grow out of the leadership inner value system but can be externally displayed predominantly as an outbound or outward attribute or both:

1. **Outbound Attributes:** These are distinctive outward-bound attributes emanating from the inner strength of the leader to support external conduct in service and relationships toward others. They form the internal core functional qualities that motivate or enhance the outward manifestation of the inside character toward others. The outbound attribute such as listening and vision, for example, are the direct results of the inner values of the leader such as patience, hearing, love, humility, or all the fruits of the spirit.

2. **Outward Attributes:** These are distinctive functional outward outer visible attributes emanating from the richness of the outbound and inner values of the leader. For example, external attributes such as Servanthood, emulation/modeling, empathy, etc. are outflows from the leader who will directly impact the follower. Outward attributes can be enriched by the outbound (inner) attributes. As shown in Figure 1, the outward attributes in general form the outer core of

functional attributes in the leader as servant leadership, but they can share some overlapping functions with the outbound attributes.

Figure 1.1. Servant leadership functional attributes

In summary, a leadership attribute is more than an ability or a characteristic; it is making those characteristics or abilities functional as part of how the leader acts (his habits) in service to others and applying those characteristics (beyond just having them) in personal and service relations to others. The character or known characteristic defines some aspects of your abilities or who you are inside— e.g. honest, humble, brave, etc. Your attribute, on the other hand, defines your habits; a display of how you use your characteristics, or the actions you exhibit toward others because of who you are inside. For example, empathy as a leadership characteristic becomes a leadership attribute if the followers can distinguish the leader's acts or habits of empathy, such as walking through with his followers in their state of suffering to bring wholeness; otherwise, it is just a characteristic or ability. Leadership attributes toward others are what impact the followers' and the organizational growth more than ability and competence.

In addressing one of the self-righteous hypocritical attributes of servitude leadership, Jesus called leader-servants to be "inside-out" leaders that reflect credibility; indeed, leaders should not appear outwardly righteous when they are full of hypocrisy and lawlessness in their hearts. He was describing "inside–out" as an authentic leadership attribute measured by the display of credibility a leadership attribute!

The measuring stick of a leader-servant is Jesus Christ. We measure ourselves unto the measure of the status of the fullness of Christ (Ephesians 4:13).

The leadership attributes of an authentic leader as a servant are encapsulated in **SERVANT/SERVING LEADERSHIP** are listed in Table 1.1, and defined in Table 1.2: *Servanthood, Emulation, Responsibility, Vision, Navigation, Adaptability, Trust, Listening, Empathy, Affection, Discipleship, Encouragement, Reproduction, Stewardship, Healing-Care, Initiation, Integrity,* and *Persuasion*. Other support attributes include *Influence, Courage, and Generosity*.

The attributes have been separated into Outward and Outbound (Inner Strength) leadership Attributes. As shown in Table 1.1, each of these attributes has three or more leadership characteristics. As such, more than 65 leadership characteristics are covered in these 20 attributes. For example, a leader's Servanthood leadership attribute is characterized by his willing servant's heart of selfless role humility, sacrifice, and submissiveness. The more these are present in a leader, the more effective the servant leadership.

Table 1.1: The functional leader-servant leadership Outbound (Inner Strength) and Outward attributes

	LEADER-SERVANT LEADERSHIP ATTRIBUTES			INNER STRENGTH ATTRIBUTES	OUTWARD ATTRIBUTES
S	Servanthood	L	Listening	Adaptability	Affection
E	Emulation	E	Empathy	Courage	Discipleship
R	Responsibility	A	Affection	Empathy	Emulation
V	Vision	D	Discipleship	Encouragement	Generosity
A	Adaptability	E	Encouragement	Initiation	Healing–Care
N	Navigation	R	Reproduction	Listening	Influence
T	Trust	S	Stewardship	Navigation	Persuasion
I	Influence	H	Healing–Care	Responsibility	Reproduction
G	Generosity	I	Initiation	Stewardship	Servanthood
C	Courage	P	Persuasion	Vision	Trust/Integrity

The list does not assume that a leader has to be excellent in all attributes or even have all of them to be an effective Leader–Servant. However, the more of these attributes the leader displays in his acts of service toward others, the more productive he or she will be, and the further his impact on the followers and organization. The table also shows that two or more attributes can share common characteristics, which can be applied or observed in different contexts. For example, a leader's ability to inspire followers can be seen in his acts of discipleship, empowerment, an.d encouragement attributes in the context in which these attributes apply. Each attribute is exhibited either as a part of the outbound inner strength attribute of a leader or a part of the outward attribute. Table 1.1 is not an exhaustive list of attributes; in fact, there are hundreds of such attributes. This is just the starting point.

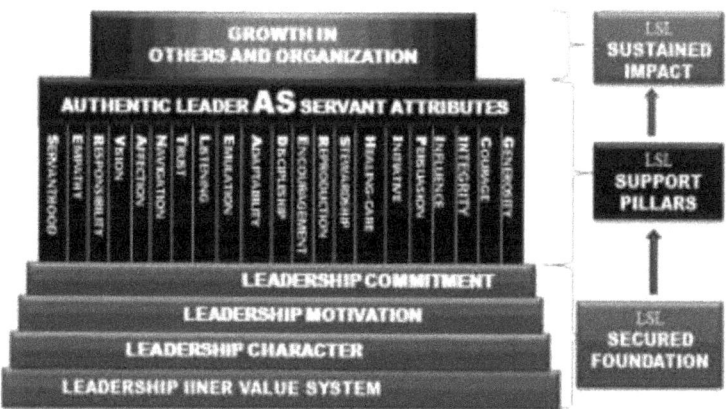

Figure 1.2: Servant leadership outward attributes (dark blue) and relationship to four foundational layers of the LSL Model

Figure 1.2 shows that the leader's attributes are shaped and secured by his four foundational layers (leadership inner value system, leadership character, motivation, and commitment). The attributes of the leader–servants are also conceptualized as the support pillars that will establish and support the personal authenticity of the leader, what the leader, does and the effectiveness of the leadership process. Thus, the attributes represent functional pillars of authentic leadership that can be learned or enriched as described in detail in the subsequent chapters. The combined effect of a secured foundation and stable support pillars will make a sustained impact on the growth of followers and the organization.

COMPARISONS WITH OTHER WORKS

The original works by Greenleaf (1970) in servant leadership [1] have been reviewed by Larry Spears (1996), who identified listening, empathy, healing, awareness, persuasion, conceptualization, foresight, stewardship, commitment to the growth of others, and building community as the ten distinguishing characteristics of servant leadership. [2] Russell (2001) has studied these attributes and have shown them to be essential in servant leadership and concluded that these qualities generally "grow out of the inner values and beliefs of individual leaders." [3] Russell and Stone (2002) extended the Greenleaf 10 attributes to 20 attributes observed in servant-leaders. These 20 attributes were categorized by these authors as either functional attributes (intrinsic characteristics of servant-leaders) or accompanying attributes (complement attributes that enhance the functional attributes).[4] The operational attributes were identified as vision, honesty, integrity, trust, modeling, service, pioneering, appreciation, and empowerment with the accompanying attributes of communication, credibility, competence, stewardship, visibility, influence, persuasion, listening, encouragement, teaching, and delegation. Only three of the attributes identified by Greenleaf were identified, and all three were accompanying attributes rather than functional. Responsibility, adaptability, affection, discipleship, navigation, and reproduction attributes which are considered critical in biblical-based servant leadership in my LSL model are not covered by Russell and Greenleaf. As shown in the description of the attributes in Table 1.2, most of the attributes reported by Russell and Stone (2002)[5] or Greenleaf [1] can be seen either in the twenty attributes or their associated characteristics. Integrity and honesty for example are leadership characteristics of trust and other attributes rather than an independent attributes. I take the position that servant leadership attributes are functional attributes in acts of duty to others and emanate from the inner value system of the leader.

CHAPTER 1
UNDERSTANDING LEADERSHIP ATTRIBUTES

Table 1.2: Description of the functional leader-servant outward leadership attributes and associated principles and characteristics

Leader–Servant Leadership Attributes	Principles of Leadership Attributes	Leadership Characteristics
Affection: *This is the combined love-based works toward providing the essential help or services for the spiritual growth or survival of another person. .* (Chapter 2)	*Affection flows from a person to produce positive emotions for the well-being of another person*	Kindness Compassion Practical Love Affective signs Appreciation
Discipleship: *This is the combined acts of personally developing, intentionally equipping, and attentively empowering growth in others to reproduce a heart of service.* (Chapter 3)	*Discipleship transforms and empowers followers for service leadership that grows communities.*	Inspiring Shepherding Equipping Developing Empowering
Emulation: *This is the combined acts of initiating an authentic servant attitude as a model of service worthy of following* (Chapter 4)	*A great leader-servant outwardly and positively inspires a pattern of good works for others to follow.*	Inspiration Motivation Initiation Model Following
Generosity: *This is the combined acts of freely sharing with and giving to others as an act of kindness, without expectation of reward or return to him.* (Chapter 5)	*Generosity is an outward measure of the level of sacrifice, what is shared, or the impact a giving makes, not just the size of the giving.*	Sharing Giving Kindness Affection Love
Healing-Care: *This is the combined acts of providing comfort and empathy to make others whole emotionally and spiritually along with tending to the follower's physical and mental well-being.* (Chapter 6)	*Comforting others in any trouble with the comfort with which we are comforted by God, brings healing - wholeness.*	Self-Healing Empathy Reconciliation Comfort Relational
Influence: *This is the combined acts of positively affecting desired change in conduct,*	*The true measure of leadership success in affecting*	Model Positive attitude Authority

performance, and relational connections toward others-centered course of action or service. (Chapter 7)	desired change in conduct, performance, and relational connections in others is influence	Connection Wisdom Intelligence,
Persuasion: This is the combined acts of communicating perspective to connect, challenge, and convince with a compelling purpose to convert others to a new position. (Chapter 8)	*The means of transforming others to a new perspective is through empathetic persuasion*	Connecting Challenging Communicating Convincing Converting Encouraging
Reproduction: This is the combined acts of developing your leadership qualities in others and releasing them as successors to continue a greater mission. (Chapter 9)	*Great leaders produce successors for legacy and greater courses as an expected product of an effective leadership reproduction.*	Selecting Mentoring Equipping Empowering Releasing
Servanthood: This is the combined acts of humility, willingness, and intentionality in service to others through selfless sacrifice and submission as a servant. (Chapter 10)	*A leader-servant is most qualified to lead when most ready to serve as a servant for the growth of others. The role of a leader is to serve as a servant*	Servant's heart Humility Sacrifice Service Willingness Submissiveness
Trust: This is the combined acts of positive display of character, competence, credibility, and shared relational connections that produce assured trust-confidence of the trustee in the trusted. (Chapter 11)	*True leadership trust produces assured trustee's confidence and readiness to follow based on the credibility, competence, and shared relational connections of the trusted.*	Character Competence Integrity Credibility Confidence

PRINCIPLE OF LEADERSHIP ATTRIBUTE

In the context of servant leadership, a leadership attribute is a level above the leadership characteristic or trait of a leader. The principle of leadership attribute states that every leadership attribute has a set of distinguishing characteristics that make up the inward or outward display of the attribute. The principle reflects the essential designed purpose or outcome of the attribute or the inevitable consequence of the effective practice of the attribute. Thus, the principle of leadership attribute is a concise statement about the fundamental truth, value, or belief about the attribute in a leadership situation; it is a statement that establishes an idea about the outcome of the attribute for guiding the practical application of the attribute and its characteristics. I will postulate and frame each principle as an additive function of the characteristics of the attribute. A statement of each principle is quoted at the beginning or below the title of each chapter. It is yet to be experimentally proven if the attribute is a linear or some other non-linear function of these characteristics as variables. It is expected, however, that each character will contribute to the effectiveness of the attribute in varying degrees.

AUTHENTIC LEADERSHIP ATTRIBUTES

At a personal level, attributes are the value-based inside-out moral leadership assets that can be related to the authenticity of a leader-servant. The complexity of defining authenticity has been noted in the literature. The subject of authentic leadership is well covered in the works of Terry (1993),[5] George (2003),[6] and Shair and Eilam (2005).[7] All appear to agree that authenticity requires self-awareness and objective self-identity in personal and social interactions with others. In his book, *Advocacy Leadership*, Professor Gary L. Anderson offers individual, organizational, and societal perspectives on authenticity: "Authenticity, at a peculiar level, is living a life, whether in the private or professional term. This is congruent with one's espoused values; at the structural level, authenticity has to do with viewing human beings as ends in themselves, rather than means to other ends; at the public level, it is a state of affairs that is congruous with the shared political and cultural values of society."[8]

The basic tenets of these perspectives are very fitting to authenticity as a qualifying element of leader-servant leadership attributes. The attribute reflects how the followers see the leader based on the leader's distinctive features displayed through his or her actions personally, organizationally, and societally. The leader is seen as a leader-servant or serving leader because the followers see him lead as a servant from an inside-out value of others. This is what makes the leader authentic.

Authenticity means that what a leader displays outside, in personal or leadership life of service to others, and society is based on the values the leader espouses inside.

Authenticity in servant leadership can be one or two types or both: *Outbound Authenticity and Outward Authenticity*: The Outbound (outward-bound) Authenticity is the genuineness of personal honesty from your inner strength and abilities; what you say and how you act emanate from who you are or how you feel inside. It reflects the essential truth and honesty about your outward-bound inner strength.

Outward authenticity, on the other hand, describes the truthfulness of your credibility and honesty displayed outward in relation to others; your *outer* visible behavior or how you act outwardly towards others reflects exactly your true intentions.

While *outward* authenticity is the visible *outer* indicator of the truth of who you are inside, *outbound* authenticity is outward-bound attribute from the inside of who you are. Credibility in this context is the influence a leader has to attract believability, trustworthiness, and authenticity; it is the believability, trustworthiness, and authenticity of who you are inside and outside.

A key element of personal authenticity is that it is seen or measured in the context of societal, cultural, and organizational interactions. In that context, achieving individual authenticity becomes a challenge since it is influenced by social factors and dispositions of individuals who usually depend on liberal and organizational realities. However, for leader-servant leadership, the leader can face those changing times by remaining focused on his key Biblical-based principles or *Leadership Inner Value System*. Thus, I am interested in authenticity as an essential element of effective Leader-servant leadership attributes or Leader-servant leadership attributes as drivers of leadership authenticity. With that in mind, the first critical element of authenticity in practicing or developing efficient leader-servant leadership attributes is inside-out self-examination relative to the people served rather than the organization. You may ask yourself: What will be my response when the people I lead act or react in a certain way, will it be negative or positive? What are my strengths and vulnerabilities at those times?

Professor Yacobi in his post, "Elements of Human Authenticity," noted that since "the self-arise attribute emerges from interactions between self, others, and the environment in a complex society and world, there may co-exist multiple complicated identities depending on place and context." [9] He went on to identify the following <u>essential elements of personal authenticity</u>: self-awareness, unbiased self-examination, accurate self-knowledge, reflective judgment, personal responsibility, and integrity, genuineness, and humility, empathy for others, understanding of others, optimal utilization of feedback from others. All of these are covered under the leadership attributes or characteristics shown in Table 1.2.

Bill George, in his book, *Authentic Leadership*, takes the position that to be an authentic leader; a person must have the following essential characteristics: [10]

- Behavior based on value: He must understand his own values and exhibit behavior to others based on those values;
- He must not compromise his values in difficult situations but could use the situation to strengthen personal values in those situations.
- Passion from a clear purpose: Be self-aware of who he is, where he is going, and the right thing to do.
- Compassion from the heart: He must lead from a compassionate heart that allows them to be sensitive to the plight and needs of others,
- Connectedness from a relationship; he must be relationally connected with people he leads,
- Consistency from the self-disciple: He must demonstrate self-discipline to remain calm, collected, and consistent in a stressful situation.

Modeled after the elements above, Table 1.3 lists six essential characteristics of authenticity for servant leadership. These fundamental characteristics cover the five identified above and can also be aligned with the leadership characteristics in Table 1.2. Each attribute in Table 1.2 is expected to pass the personal authenticity test in Tables 1.3, 1.4. In a survey of 132 Christian leaders, seventy-four percent (74%) of them agreed that they always or frequently exhibit servant leadership attributes. [11] Thus, a pass of the outward authenticity test means that a pure leader must demonstrate 70% or more of these essential elements of this legitimacy. (That is, 70% YES in the assessment questions in Tables 1.3, 1.4).

It needs to be noted, however, that a secular leader could be authentic and still lack some of the essential servant leadership attributes or characteristics such as selflessness, servanthood, and love-motivated servant attitudes of a leader-servant. Effective leader-servants are authentic leaders and personal authenticity is an essential element of leader-servant leadership. The key test for leader-servant authenticity is the quality of his inside-out value and personal character. What is most important is a change from the inside-out.

Table 1.3: The test of essential elements of personal inner strength authenticity in servant leadership

	Elements of Inner Strength Authenticity	Inner Strength (Outbound) Authenticity Assessment Questions	YES / NO
1	Personal inside-out value-based behavior	Are your personal inside-out values aligned with acts of service and behavior outside?	1
		Are you honest to yourself in relation to your inner strengths and abilities?	2
2	Inside-out Self-Awareness	Do you have unbiased self-examination, and accurate self-knowledge of who you are inside-out?	3
		Do you know your inner strength and weaknesses in relation to the good you want to show as an outward attribute?	4
3	Inside-out Empathy-Compassion	Do you know and feel from your inside what you want for your followers?	5
		Are you motivated to empathize, based on your inside feelings?	6
4	Inside-out Connection with followers	Do you feel deep, personal, and spiritual connection with your followers?	7
		Does what you say and how you act reflect how you feel when you relate to others?	8
5	Inside-out Emotional Self-regulation	Do you have difficulty controlling your emotion in order to remain calm in a stressful situation?	9
		Are you always able to comfort yourself?	10
6	Inside-out Authenticity Feedback	Do your followers see your inside-out value from your outside behavior?	11
		Will your followers feel that what you say you are is congruent with how you act?	12
#YESs____; # NOs____: Outbound Authenticity: YES/ 12-----%			

CHAPTER 1
UNDERSTANDING LEADERSHIP ATTRIBUTES

Table 1.4: The test of essential elements of personal outward authenticity in servant leadership			
	Elements of Personal Outward Authenticity	Personal Outward Authenticity Assessment Questions	YES or NO
1	Personal value-based outward behavior	Are your personal values and beliefs aligned with your acts of service and behavior toward others?	1
		Do you live out your life according to your beliefs?	2
2	Personal Self-Awareness	Do you have clarity of your personal vision and purpose?	3
		Does what you know about yourself accurately describe what others say?	4
3	Personal Outward Empathy-Compassion	Do you apply how you feel to what your followers need?	5
		Do you lead from a compassionate heart and are you sensitive to the plight and needs of others?	6
4	Personal Connection with followers	Do you feel deep, personal connection with your followers?	7
		Does your outward action toward others reflect exactly your true intentions?	8
5	Outward Emotional Self-regulation	Do you have difficulty controlling your emotions to remain calm in a stressful situation?	9
		Does your evaluation of your value of others agree with how valued they feel?	10
6	Personal Authenticity Feedback	Do your followers see your outward acts as true and honest?	11
		Can your followers see other-centeredness in 70% or more of your attributes?	12
#YESs____; # NOs____: Outbound Authenticity: YES/ 12-----%			

ALS ADAPTABILITY LEADERSHIP
ATTRIBUTES, PRINCIPLES & PRINCIPLES

SUMMARY 1
UNDERSTANDING LEADERSHIP PROCESS

Before starting this exercise, please read and follow the instruction in the preface of this workbook. Answers to these questions are contained in this chapter. Completion of these exercises after reading the chapter should take 60-90 minutes.

Discovering the Leadership Attributes

1. What is your alternative definition of leadership? In learning to lead, how would you differentiate the following elements:
   a. Leadership.
   b. Leader as servant leadership.
   c. Leadership characteristics.
   d. Leadership attributes.
2. What are the key differences between the Leader as Servant and the Servant as Leader Leadership philosophies?
3. What was the original source of the Servant as Leader (SL)? What was the original source of Leader as Servant (LS)?
4. What is the key framework of a Leader as a Servant Leadership?
5. Authenticity in servant leadership can be one or two types or both *Outbound Authenticity and Outward Authenticity*: Describe a time when you displayed:
   a. The Outbound (outward-bound)— *outbound* authenticity is outward-bound attribute from the inside of who you are.
   b. *The Outward Authenticity*—*outward* authenticity is the visible *outer* indicator of the truth of who you are inside,
6. Describe the key elements of personal authenticity seen or measured in the context of societal, cultural, and organizational interactions.
7. How are the essential characteristics of authentic leader in leadership process in challenging times.
8. How much of a leader-servant are you? Take the personal leader-servant audit in Table 1.5 to self-assess your effectiveness.
9. Based on the questions in Table 1.5, can you identify each of the twenty attributes? What ones did you score 3 ("sometimes") or less than 3? Review and learn and commit to work to improve.

CHAPTER 1
UNDERSTANDING LEADERSHIP ATTRIBUTES

Table 1.5. Leader As Servant-Leadership Audit

A servant-leader in his leadership position purposefully choses to serve and inspire acts of service in others by his example. Select and circle best answer to questions
1=Never; 2=Almost never; 3=Sometimes; 4=Frequently; 5 =Always

	Servant Leadership assessment questions	Circle no				
1	I am willing and other-centered, and readily chose to serve others as a servant for their personal growth	1	2	3	4	5
2	I model others-centered attitude in my service and relationships and inspire same for others to follow	1	2	3	4	5
3	I have a sense of obligation, willingness, and accountability for the service towards others	1	2	3	4	5
4	I have the foresightedness to specify in the present view what others' growth should be in a given future	1	2	3	4	5
5	I work toward providing the essential help or services for the spiritual growth or survival of the others;	1	2	3	4	5
6	I provide the needed purposeful course of action for how to chart the course to for my followers.	1	2	3	4	5
7	I display external credibility and a strong sense of character based on values, beliefs, and competence;	1	2	3	4	5
8	In communication, I attentively perceive and hear what is communicated, reflectively listen to understand and to be understood	1	2	3	4	5
9	I walk through with others in their state (suffering, emotions, etc.) in a way that provides the needed care and well-being	1	2	3	4	5
10	I have a measure of self-secured flexibility to adapt appropriate attitude to serve all people in different situations	1	2	3	4	5
11	I personally develop, intentionally equip, and attentively nurture spiritually growth in others	1	2	3	4	5
12	My act of bravery instills in others the courage and confidence to follow or persevere in a course of action	1	2	3	4	5
13	I develop my leadership qualities in others as successors to continue in a purposeful mission	1	2	3	4	5
14	I manage, maintain,, and account for all resources entrusted to me and being responsible for the difference my acts make	1	2	3	4	5
15	As a care-giver, I act to comfort and make others whole emotionally	1	2	3	4	5
16	When I see a need, I originate a vision and action, and stay committed to meet that need and desired change	1	2	3	4	5

ALS ADAPTABILITY LEADERSHIP
ATTRIBUTES, PRINCIPLES & PRINCIPLES

17	I display a holistic view of an issue to inform, transform or convert others to my view through empathetic persuasion	1	2	3	4	5
18	I freely share what I have sacrificially as an act of kindness to others, without expectation of reward in return	1	2	3	4	5
19	My act of influence is to affect the actions, behavior, opinions, etc., of others based on trust, credibility and relationship	1	2	3	4	5
20	In the face challenges and danger, I act with bravery to overcome fear and take a stand with strength and conviction	1	2	3	4	5
Score Range	Add up the numbers in each column (Total Score____) Check and Understand the key areas to work on					
81-100	Strong Leader-Servant; keep it up, go and train others.					
66-80	Above average Leader-Servant; work 25% of key areas					
50-65	Average but developing; need to work on 50% of key areas					
34-49	Below average leader; work on 75% of key areas					
<34	Not a Leader-Servant; need training in all areas					

CHAPTER 2
ADAPTABILITY LEADERSHIP ATTRIBUTE

Flexibility overcomes rigidity in new and changing situations.

Adaptability is an inner strength characteristic that is visibly missing in most other leadership models and yet is essential in Servant leadership. We must respond to changing needs or situations. Jesus modeled adaptability in the different methods with which he ministered and healed people. God showed Moses adaptability when he empowered him to use the rod in his hand as an instrument for the mission ahead of him. I have moved around quite a bit in my 25 years as a faculty member and as a senior administrator. Each move presented a distinctive set of expectations, situations, people, cultures, opportunities, and resources. In serving the African Christian Fellowship in different U.S. states, I have consistently realized that the variables in any two situations are always different.

A friend, in fact, my college freshman roommate, was once an Executive Senior Vice-President worldwide of this international bank. He had climbed up to the highest ladder of leadership in his division with comfort and personal fringe benefits (official cars and driver, cook, stewards, bodyguards, and company quarters in major cities) that most of us would not give up. He stepped down from that position into a full-time ministry as a pastor of a local church he founded with a small congregation, and receives little or no financial enumeration.

While at a ministers' conference, I was shocked when I saw him listed as a pastor. To put this in context, my friend was not a Christian when we were roommates for over 20 years from this time. In fact, he was anti-anything that was Christian and gave me the greatest challenge in Christian witnessing each time I tried to introduce him to Christ. He was always ready with questions that would make any young Christian in the Lord as I was, look stupid. Naturally, when I saw his name on the list, my first response was disbelief, knowing this my friend, how anti-religious he was, and remembering the position I knew he was holding when I last saw him. I simply could not imagine how he could adapt from his so high position to this low one; at least that was my thought. I could not dismiss his name from my mind. So, I called the number listed with the name. And behold, it was him. My first set of questions to him was how did this happen? When did this happen? How are you dealing with the new change in position and comfort? I wanted to know what it was that allowed him to adjust to his new situation. His response was as shocking as it was humbling. His short answer was, "The things of the world could only temporarily 'gratify' but only the service and things of God are satisfying to me. Today, I am building people and leading them to 'bank' and 'invest' their lives in the work of God. There is an absolute satisfaction even though I am not receiving any financial enumeration, and we struggle to make ends meet." He felt more *self-secured* in God and chose to count the things of the world he had (that most leaders would go for) as nothing, compared to the service of God. I sensed absolute *humility* in him and the *flexibility* to adapt to the situation he has intentional chose. He has counted the change as a sacrifice for the greater good.

As the saying goes, "change is the constant of life," how do you handle or prepare for such an inevitable variable of life? The last time you were faced with a change or situation unfamiliar to you, what attitude did you exhibit? This chapter will attempt to give answers and meanings to these and personal reflective questions to discover the distinguishing characteristics of Leadership Adaptability Attribute. Functional definitions of Leadership Adaptability attributes and principles will be provided based on the identified characteristics. Readers will benefit from numerous techniques, personal examples, empirical case studies, and applications of the concepts.

SERVANT LEADERSHIP ADAPTABILITY ATTRIBUTE

The U.S. Army discovered adaptability trait as one key element of leadership. According to the Army training Handbook, adaptability is "an individual's ability to recognize changes in the environment, identify the critical elements of the new situation, and trigger changes accordingly to meet new requirements." [11] The major characteristics of adaptability according to this handbook include the ability to:

- Scan the environment.
- Derive the key characteristics of the situation.
- Be aware of what it will take to perform in the changed environment.
- Be comfortable entering unfamiliar environments with a proper frame of mind.
- Assess the situation quickly and determine the skills needed to deal with it.
- Serve as an agent of change.
- Work to influence the course of the organization.
- Use several different methods to influence the organization.
- Enter different situations using distinctive manners depending on the situation.
- Handle ambiguity comfortably.
- Remain flexible and innovative.
- Be resourceful; be ready to face the challenges at hand with the resources available.
- Be a passionate learner.
- Handle multiple demands, shifting priorities, and rapid change smoothly.
- See each change as an opportunity rather than a liability.

Although the Army's leadership principles are elements of the power control model at the very core of leadership in the Army, some of the qualities that comprise adaptability are truly similar to what one finds in Servant leadership. Let us look at Paul talking about his quality of adaptability. He writes:

> *For though I am free from all men, I have made myself a servant to all, that I might win the more; and to the Jews, I became as a Jew, that I might win Jews; to those who are under the law, as under the law, that I might win those who are under the law; to those who are without law, as without law (not being without law toward God but under law toward Christ), that I might win those who are without law; to the weak, I became as weak, that I might win the weak. I have become all things to all men that I might by all means save some. Now, this I do for the gospel's sake, that I may be partaker of it with you* (1 Corinthians 9:19-24).

The above passage is a masterpiece description of an adaptable leader. The Apostle Paul, though free from all men, made himself "a servant to all"—" as a Jew," "as under the law," "as without the law." and "as weak" …to by all means save some in Christ.

Just as in the Army's definition, an adaptable leader-servant has the self-awareness and confidence to "trigger changes accordingly to meet new requirements" [11] Compared to the Army list and the scripture above; we can group the characteristics of adaptability into three adaptability drivers: *Self-Security, Flexibility,* and *Compassion,* and summarized in Table 2.1.

Table 2.1: Characteristics of Adaptability Attribute

Self-security
Self-secured and self-controlled in unfamiliar situations
Discern ambiguity presented by other cultures, practices, and perspectives
Self-secured to make the sacrifice to be all things to all to save some
Self-secured to feel satisfied in the service of others as service to God
Flexibility
Flexible in his approach to serve all people, but fixed in his mission to influence change in different people in changing conditions.
Flexible to self-regulate his emotions to empathize with others.
Flexibility in personal preferences in serving others
Flexible in toward others rights than his rights

Compassion
Compassion to enter into different situations depending on the situation.
Readiness to face challenges at hand with the resources available.
Self-aware of conditions outside his comfort zone with a proper frame of mind.
Concerned about changes and conditions of others and environment in which he serves

PRINCIPLE OF LEADERSHIP ADAPTABILITY ATTRIBUTE

From the above characteristics, I posit the following:

Servant Leadership Adaptability Attribute is the combined acts of self-secured flexibility and compassion to serve all people without compromising their core values.

Adaptability attribute requires the ability to be self-aware of the needs of others, self-secured enough, and flexible to adapt to unfavorable conditions to meet those needs. These abilities will lead adaptability only in the absence of rigidity in the attitude of the leader. This principle is stated as follows:

Servant leadership adaptability principle: Flexibility overcomes rigidity in new and changing situations.

The relationship between the three characteristics: — *self-security, flexibility, and compassion* is illustrated in Figure 2 and expressed as:

SELF- SECURITY + FLEXIBILITY + COMPASSION = ADAPTABILITY

The principle means that rigidity as an attitude ceases when there is flexibility.

Figure 5.1 illustrates the logic of the model of the leader-servant's adaptability attribute. The model shows that the three qualities of adaptability can occur in any direction and can be related to each other through a continuous sequence of stages, actions, tasks, or behaviors.

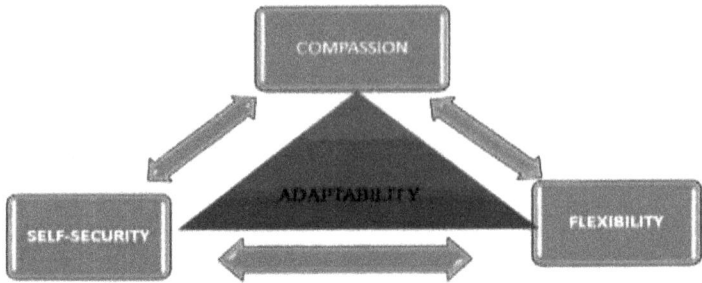

Figure 2: Servant leadership adaptability –attribute model

SUMMARY 2
ADAPTABILITY LEADERSHIP ATTRIBUTE

Before starting this exercise, please read and follow the instruction in the preface of this workbook. Answers to these questions are contained in this chapter. Completion of these exercises after reading the chapter should take 60-90 minutes.

Understanding Adaptability Leadership Attribute

1. Define adaptability. How did Jesus model that definition in His service to humanity?
2. As the saying goes, "change is the constant of life," how can adaptability attribute help you to handle or prepare for such an inevitable variable of life?

Developing Adaptability Leadership Attribute

1. According to the Army training Handbook, adaptability is "an individual's ability to recognize changes in the environment, identify the critical elements of the new situation, and trigger changes accordingly to meet new requirements." Fifteen major characteristics of adaptability were listed. List five or more of those that are not power-control base that you believe you adopt in your lived experiences
2. What does Apostle Paul teach about adaptability
(1 Corinthians 9:19-24)?
3. Comparing Apostle Paul with the Army list, group the characteristics of adaptability into three adaptability drivers

CHAPTER 2
ADAPTABILITY LEADERSHIP ATTRIBUTE

Understanding the Principle of Adaptability Leadership Attribute

1. From the above characteristics, I posit the following:
2. Define Servant *Leadership Adaptability Attribute*
3. *State the* principle of adaptability
4. State the additive law of adaptability
5. How are the three qualities of adaptability be related to each other

Practicing Adaptability Attribute

1. What meaning or lesson can you frame from the experience of reading this chapter?
2. List the characteristics of your Adaptability leadership attributes.
3. How much of the acts of adaptability as an attribute do you display?
4. Take the leadership adaptability attribute audit in Table A-II.1
5. With reference to adaptability leadership attribute, what take-away, meaning or lesson can you frame to improve your adaptability in a leadership process?
6. Write a commitment statements of your plan to improve in your acts of adaptability attributes.

ALS ADAPTABILITY LEADERSHIP
ATTRIBUTES, PRINCIPLES & PRINCIPLES

Table AII.1 Leadership Adaptability Attribute Audit

Servant Leadership Adaptability Attribute is the combined acts of self-secured flexibility and compassion to serve all people without compromising his core values. Assess the quality of your acts of adaptability attribute by inserting an X below the number that best describes your response to each statement.

Item	Acts of Adaptability Attribute Check 1= Always; 2= Frequently; 3= Sometimes; 4= Almost Never; 5= Never	1	2	3	4	5
1	I am not fixed on process but adopt whatever method will bring wholeness to the people					
2	I am flexible to accommodate conditions outside my comfort zone					
3	I am flexible in making the sacrifices and changes necessary to meet the needs of others					
4	I am flexible in my approach to serve all people, but fixed in the mission to influence change					
5	I know what matters most in lives of followers and adapt to appropriate behavior to add value.					
6	I show compassion as an element of the adaptability attribute?					
7	I take appropriate action to bring wholeness to another person.					
8	My sense of self-security is strong in entering an unfamiliar environment outside my comfort zone					
9	I am able to discern ambiguity presented by new environment, practices, and perspectives					
10	I am self-secured and feel satisfied in the service of others as service to God					
	Add up your rating in each column					
Score Range	Guide and Explanation of Score: understand the areas you need to develop	Total score=				

10-17: Great adaptable leadership; keep it up!
18-25: Above Average adaptable leader; need to work on 25% of the areas
26-33: Average adaptable leader; need to need to work on 50% of the areas;
34-41: Below average-poor adaptable leader; need to work on 75% of the areas
42-50: Not an adaptable leader; need to work on all the areas

CHAPTER 3
DEVELOPING ADAPTABILITY– SELF-SECURITY

Adaptability-self-security attitude is the quality of a leader's self-security that builds his inner strength and allows him to enter an unfamiliar environment outside his comfort zone with confidence that he will not be compromised in any way. This is important because not everyone can seek to be all things to all people and emerge intact. You have to be sure of yourself to be with certain people, such as lawless drug dealers, without compromising your integrity; or to be able to enter a brothel to witness prostitutes without falling into temptation, or go to club houses without indulging in one of the vices or even showing a desire to do so. The Apostle Paul entered into unfamiliar places as the inhabitants. This means that his primary purpose was to win them for Christ but without adopting their qualities. It is a one-way influence, and only self-secured leaders can enter into such a dragon's lair. Insecure leaders should not walk into the forest where lions feed. Sister Patience Obih of the African Christian Fellowship always reminded leaders that "Mortal men should not tread the floor where only Angels fall." The following strategies should help self-secure leaders in acts of adaptability:

Develop self-security awareness

Self-security awareness is the level of consciousness that increases the leader's security and confidence in himself to step out without hurting or compromising himself. Adaptable leader-servants are aware of themselves—their strengths and weaknesses—and what it will take to meet the needs of each follower effectively. He disciplines those areas of his life that need to be in conformity with what is needed in his service. The ability and courage to overcome temptation in unfamiliar environments is the mark of a secure leader. Many leaders fail before they realize what caused them to fail, whereas successful leaders identify what which can make them fail at the beginning of their leadership pyramid and avoid those pitfalls.

Develop a sense of self-security

A sense of self-security is being self-aware and intelligent of the characteristics of the unfamiliar environment. For a leader to effectively adapt to an unfamiliar environment, he must be aware of the challenges in the environment and what it will take to meet the needs of the people effectively. He must take appropriate steps to understand the characteristics of the people he will be serving and must be able to match those characteristics to his abilities. You cannot avoid being taken by surprise. Paul had to know the people before he proceeded to "be as" them.

Develop a self-secured frame of mind

Have a self-secured frame of mind for adaptability. A secure frame of the mind prepares the leader for possible challenges in any situation. It allows a leader to control his thoughts to focus on the mission. An adaptable leader-servant has a secured proper frame of mind to provide the right perspective outside his comfort zone. Unfamiliar places of ministry or people to serve to require that the leader be self-secured, and he must also have the right frame of mind to avoid fear and distraction. Unfamiliar environments, such as a "war zone," can present a state of suffering or difficulties, and a leader must not be "ignorant of the devices of the enemy." To win people outside your cultural territory, you must be aware of the dos and don'ts in that culture. You must be able to negotiate your way around the culture with the right frame of mind. When missionaries go on field trips, their training and preparation usually include awareness of certain cultural norms and how to adapt to the new environment. The frame of mind you need for service in an Islamic environment or community is different from what you need for a general non-Christian community. For example, an Islamic community may have a strong Islamic culture, beliefs, and values that might be close to Christian values while a non-Christian (non-Islamic) believing culture may be open but ignorant of the Biblical-based value system. Each presents a different frame of adaptation and a set of challenges.

SUMMARY 3
DEVELOPING ADAPTABILITY–SELF-SECURITY

Before starting this exercise, please read and follow the instruction in the preface of this workbook. Answers to these questions are contained in this chapter. Completion of these exercises after reading the chapter should take 60-90 minutes.

Understanding the Acts of Adaptability -Self security Attribute

1. Define Adaptability-self-security attribute. What is the role of quality Adaptability-self-security attribute

Practicing the Acts of Adaptability -Self security Attribute

1. What meaning or lesson can you frame from the experience of reading this chapter?
2. In developing self-security awareness as a strategy, what is Self-security awareness and what must leaders be aware of in service to others and why?
3. In developing a sense of self-security as strategy, what is sense of self-security and how is this important for an unfamiliar environment,
4. Developing a self-secured frame of mind is an adaptability strategy. What is the role of a secure frame of the mind.
5. How does this strategy hel To win people outside your cultural territory.
6. Practicing the Acts of Adaptability-self-security. **Adaptability-self-security** attitude is the quality of a leader's self-security that builds the inner strength that allows him to enter an unfamiliar environment outside his comfort zone with confidence that he will not be compromised in any way.
    a. What is the implication of this attitude in being "all things to all people?"
    b. How can you be secured in an environment that is outside the norm?

CHAPTER 4
BUILDING ADAPTABILITY-FLEXIBILTY

Adaptability-flexibility attitudes are flexible service-orientated behaviors adopted to meet the needs of followers or to accommodate conditions outside one's comfort zone with a proper frame of mind. The key essence of adaptability in servant leadership is to be "all things to all men" and be flexible in all situations in serving others. Flexibility means not being double-minded. It is being single-minded but adjusting to appropriate strategies for the specific mission. Flexibility also avoids being rigid and attempting to use the same method to serve others in different environments. Flexibility means not changing your mind in the middle of a mission, but rather adapting to appropriate frame of mind to remain fixed on the goal. It is not flipping from one position to the other to serve your purpose (as we see in politicians) but is having a people-centered purpose and compassion to give up your comfort to serve other peoples' needs. The following flexibility strategies will increase a leader's adaptability attribute:

Develop flexible approaches to service

Because no one method first, adaptability means being flexible in your approaches in service to others depending on the person, situations, environments, limitations, etc. The adaptable leader-servants need to be flexible in their approach to meet different people's needs, but be fixed in their core mission. Different ministries that serve the needs of people require different approaches depending on the people, demographics, and geographical locations. For the Apostle Paul, this meant the Jews, people under the law, without the law, and the weak. Each group had different needs and therefore, required different approaches. The first action of a leader-servant is to try to understand the people being served, be aware of their specific needs, and be open to adjusting the approach even if it is toward an unfamiliar follower and environment. The leader forgoes the right to be selective or discriminatory. The lead needs to be aware of cultural differences when attempting to cross-culturally communicate in order to win over or serve people different from your culture. Rigidity in approaches will only set the leader apart from the people he or she intends to serve.

Develop flexibility in sacrifice to service

Adaptable leader-servants are flexible in making the sacrifices and changes necessary to meet the needs of others and the organization. We meet several people from different walks of life who have an incredible sense of flexibility in handling change. Businessman Jack Welch, the CEO of General Electric, is one example. At a time when GE was struggling for growth, Welch looked at the current structure of GE and their business functions that had not changed for decades. He knew that GE could reach new heights if he tried a different kind of revolution. Jack Welch chose to change the company's way of thinking. According to Jeffrey A. Krames in his book, *The Welch Way*, Welch's goal and passion was to make GE "the world's most competitive enterprise." [12] Welch's self-proclaimed revolution meant waging "war" on GE's old ways of doing things and reinventing the company from top to bottom. He developed the idea of a "boundary-less" organization, where everyone is empowered to share and bring new ideas rather than depending on decisions in the board room with just top executives. He empowered and set his workers free to contribute ideas by promising that he would listen to them. The result was that GE emerged from a period of stagnation and became a successful giant, mainly because members of his team followed his lead. Jack also followed through on whatever he said he would do. "This is a key to the Welch success," wrote Jeffrey A. Krames in *The Welch Way*. "He had great energy, sparked others, had an incredible competitive spirit, and had a record of execution that was second to none. Had he been lacking in any of the traits he espoused, he would not have commanded such acclaim." [12] Just as in the approaches used to meet those needs; different levels of sacrifice are needed for different challenges in the mission to serve others.

CHAPTER 4
DEVELOPING ADAPTABILITY–FLEXIBILITY

SUMMARY 4
DEVELOPING ADAPTABILITY–FLEXIBITY

Before starting this exercise, please read and follow the instruction in the preface of this workbook. Answers to these questions are contained in this chapter. Completion of these exercises after reading the chapter should take 60-90 minutes.

Understanding the Acts of Adaptability-Flexibility

1. What is an Adaptability-flexibility attitude?; what does Flexibility mean with respect to service to others?.
2. What is the key essence of adaptability in servant leadership?
3. How do the - flexible behaviors of a leader meet the needs of followers or accommodate conditions outside the comfort zone with a proper frame of mind?

Practicing the Acts of Adaptability-Flexibility

1. What meaning or lesson can you frame from the experience of reading this chapter?
2. What are the roles of flexible approaches and how do you develop flexible approaches to service?
3. Different ministries that serve the needs of people require different approaches depending on the people, demographics, and geographical locations. What strategies did Apostle Paul adapt?
4. What is the negative impact of rigidity in your acts?
5. Developing flexibility in sacrifice to service is an effective strategy in making the sacrifices and changes necessary to meet the needs of others and the organization. What are the different levels of sacrifice needed for different challenges in the mission to serve others?
6. What strategies can leaders use to increase a leader's adaptability attributes?

CHAPTER 5
DEVELOPING ADAPTABILITY–COMPASSION

Adaptability-compassion is the leader's inner strength and ability to know what is worth dying for and adapting appropriate behavior to add value to people's lives. Compassion is a key element of the adaptability attribute because it provides the passion that allows the leader to be flexible in adapting his or her behaviors or personal assets to be "all things to all people."

The key element of compassion in this respect is empathy for the suffering of others and selflessness in taking appropriate action to alleviate that suffering for the well-being of that other person. Thus, compassion is at the top of the pyramid of adaptable leaders and serves as an inner driver for leaders' passion to take action to serve others. Some of Jesus' models of adaptability can be seen in his method of healing people. He adopted healing physical touches of the sick in the areas where they were hurting, whether it was their ears, eyes, or hands. In some cases, He allowed the sick to touch Him, "And as many as touched Him were made well" (Mark 6:56). In other cases, He healed people through compassion, by speaking the Word, being alone with the sick or dead, as He did when He raised Lazarus from the dead. He continuously gauged people's needs and adapted to the appropriate method to accomplish the mission or impact people the most. The following are examples of acts of compassionate adaptability in a leader-servant:

Develop compassion-empathy

Developing compassionate empathy begins with cultivating the desire for compassion toward others. Compassionate empathy is the empathy that communicates passion to care for the suffering of followers or others. An adaptable leader-servant will expend himself cultivating the desire to alleviate another's suffering by adopting an attitude for empathetic perception. He must be compassionate enough to enter and walk with the care receiver through the hurting experiences. Compassionate empathy allows us to adapt our temperament and sensitivity to ease the hurts of others for their well-being; then, the leader can bring appropriate healing without adding to the hurt. Compassionate emphatic leaders are consistently empathetic and can easily adjust their attitude to forge positive connections with others in need, even if that other person is negative. Because adaptable leaders are compassionately flexible, they are able to create a bridge to ease the suffering of others. Compassionate empathy makes leaders "high on people" and allows them to make appropriate adjustments to serve anyone. Leader-servants need to be compassionate empathizers to adapt appropriately to serve all people in need.

Develop compassion-selflessness

Leader-servants are called to cultivate the desire for compassion-selflessness. Compassion- selflessness is people-centered selfless acts of concern for the welfare of others. Rather than spending themselves and their energies on their own needs and comfort, leader-servants spend themselves — and make whatever sacrifice is required — to meet the needs of others. Selfless acts are born of compassion and sympathy. Compassionate selflessness equips leader-servants in developing people-centered missions with the mind to give their lives to a purpose that counts. This is the essence of Paul's ministry. To have compassionate selflessness, a leader must have the sense that the work they do is bigger than they are, and that it matters to God. They must see a loving God in suffering hearts and commit to being the person to heal that hurt. Leader-servants' depth of satisfaction comes from knowing that the mission is accomplished and that others gained from their selfless sacrifices.

Develop compassion-opportunities

Compassionate opportunity is change-driven compassion that allows the leader to see peoples' situations as opportunities for change without compromising his character. The leader is passionate enough to give up his rights and personal preferences to become an agent of change to turn various situations into opportunities for growth in the other person and to serve as an agent to influence change in the present situation of the follower. The leader's mission is to influence specific behavioral change. It may be to serve the person's health needs, spiritual needs, or material needs. For example, the need might be homelessness due to natural disasters or servant ministries to widows, and so on. A leader-servant as an agent of change must first identify the specific need or change he wants to influence and adapt his resources and frame of mind to meet those needs. His primary influence is to change the person's wholeness—physical, mental, emotional, and spiritual—wellbeing.

SUMMARY 5
DEVELOPING ADAPTABILITY–COMPASSION

Before starting this exercise, please read and follow the instruction in the preface of this workbook. Answers to these questions are contained in this chapter. Completion of these exercises after reading the chapter should take 60-90 minutes

1. What is Adaptability-compassion attitude?
2. How is Compassion a key element of the adaptability attribute and how is empathy a element of compassion in this respect? ..
3. Some of Jesus' models of adaptability can be seen in his method of healing people. What are some of the strategies he adopted and why did he use such methods. (see Mark 6:56)
4. Developing compassionate empathy as a strategy begins with cultivating the desire for compassion toward others. What are the roles of compassionate empathy in leadership?

Develop compassion-selflessness

Leader-servants are called to cultivate the desire for compassion selflessness. What is Compassion- selflessness in this context? what is the role of Compassionate selflessness as shown as essence of Paul's ministry.

Compassionate opportunity is change-driven compassion that allows the leader to see peoples' situations as opportunities for change without compromising his character. What is the leader's primary influence in this respect?

Practicing the Acts of Compassionate Adaptability

1. **Compassionate Adaptability** is the ability to know what was worth dying for and adapt appropriate behavior to add value to people.
2. What meaning or lesson can you frame from the experience of reading this chapter?
3. How do the - flexible behaviors of a leader meet the needs of followers or accommodate conditions outside the comfort zone with a proper frame of mind?
    a. How can compassion be an element of the adaptability attribute?
    b. List three strategies that a leader can use as acts of compassionate adaptability in serving others

TOPIC INDEX

About This Book, 20
Affective Compassion, 65
authentic, 22, 24
authentic leadership, 35
Authentic Leadership, 43
Authenticity, 41
Characteristics of Leadership
    Servanthood Attribute, 51
Comfort, 39
commitment, 17, 23
communication
    types of, 28
Communication, 28
Comparisons
    with other works, 38
Compassion, 26
Compassionate adaptability
    definition, 65, 67, 68
Compassionate empathy, 65, 67
Compassionate Opportunity, 66, 67
Compassionate Selflessness, 66, 67
credibility, 46
Empathy-attribute, 26
essence of adaptability, 61, 63
Flexibility, 61, 63
Flexibility-adaptability
    definition, 56, 61, 63, 68
    definition, 61
    definition, 63
Functional Definitions, 33
Initiative
    definition of, 27
inside-out, 44
Joshua, 17

law of, 40
LEADER, 26
Leader as Servant Leadership, 40
    definition, 23
Leader First., 21
Leader-as-Servant Leadership, 21
leader-servant's affection-attribute
    definition, 46
leadership, 23
Leadership Attributes, 41
Leadership Inner Value system, 23
Model, 21
Moses, 17
Navigation-attribute, 46
Personal Outward Authenticity, 45
Practicing Servant Leadership
    Adaptability, 55
process, 23
Security Awareness
    definition, 57, 59
Self-security adaptability, 57, 59
Servant, 21, 22
test
    for leader-servant authenticity, 44
    of essential elements of personal
        authenticity, 44, 45
The Leadership Influence-attribute, 39
The Principle of Leadership Empathy-
    Attribute, 26
The Principle of Leadership Adaptability
    Attribute, 25, 53
The Principle of Leadership listening-
    attribute, 28

REFERENCES

[1]Greenleaf, R. (1970). *The Servant as Leader,* Indianapolis: The Robert K. Greenleaf Center

[2]Spears, L. (1996*). "Reflections on Robert K. Greenleaf and servant-leadership."* Leadership & Organization Development Journal, 17(7), 33-35

[3]Russell, R.F. (2001). "The role of values in servant leadership." *Leadership &Organization Development Journal,* 22(2), 76-83

[4]Russell, R.F., and Stone, A.G. (2002). "A review of servant leadership attributes: developing a practical model." *Leadership & Organization Development Journal,* 23(3), 145-15

[5]Terry. R. W (1993*). Authentic Leadership: Courage In Action,* San Francisco, CA ,Jossey-Bass

[6]George, B (2003). *Authentic Leadership: Rediscovering the Secrets to Creating Lasting Value.* San Francisco, CA, Jossey-Bass

[7]Shamir, B. & Eilam, G. (2005). "What's your story? Toward a life-story approach to authentic leadership." Leadership Quarterly, 16, 395–418.

[8]Anderson, GL (2009). Advocacy Leadership: Toward a Post-Reform Agenda in Education, Routledge, New York, 41

[9]Yacobi, B.G. *"Elements of Human Authenticity."* http://www.philosophytogo.org /wordpress/?p=1945, Retrieved, July 15, 2012

[10]George, B (2003). *Authentic Leadership: Rediscovering the Secrets to Creating Lasting Value,* San Francisco, CA, Jossey-Bass

[11]U.S. Army Handbook (1973). Military Leadership

[12]Krames, J.A (2004). *The Welch Way , 24 Lessons From The World's Greatest CEO,* McGraw-Hill

www.ingramcontent.com/pod-product-compliance
Lightning Source LLC
LaVergne TN
LVHW051217070526
838200LV00063B/4939